THE OFFICIAL
SUNDERLAND AFC
ANNUAL 2026

Written by Rob Mason
Pages 50 & 51 provided by Barbara Mason
With thanks to: Kieran Regan, Kate Smith, Andrew Smithson, Keith Gregson, Mike Gibson, Barry Jackson
Designed by Mathew Whittles

A Grange Publication

© 2025. Published by Grange Communications Ltd., Edinburgh, under licence from Sunderland A.F.C.

Grange Communications Ltd., 25 Herbert Place, Dublin, D02 AY86 frontdesk@grangecommunications.co uk

Printed in Romania.

Photographs © Sunderland A.F.C, Alamy Ltd., Ian Horrocks

ISBN 978-1-917538-48-0

TRAI HUME

CONTENTS

STAT ATTACK

5

Promotion in 2025 was Sunderland's fifth promotion into the Premier League. No club have won more promotions into the Premier League, although Burnley, Leicester City, Norwich City and West Bromwich Albion have also been promoted into the Premier League on five occasions.

266

Sunderland spent 266 days in the top six last season, more than any other team.

100

Sunderland spent 100 days of last season in the top two of the Championship.

70

Anthony Patterson's crucial 70th minute Wembley save from Sheffield United's Andre Brooks in the Play-off final came in the same minute of the game as Jim Montgomery's legendary save in the 1973 FA Cup final.

150

In the home game against Watford Anthony Patterson became the 10th goalkeeper in Sunderland's history to reach 150 appearances.

4

Régis Le Bris became the fourth head coach / manager to start his reign at Sunderland with an away win. Denis Smith, Roy Keane and Steve Bruce are the others.

134

Sunderland won their first three league games without conceding a goal for the first time ever in their 134 years as a league club.

4

A fourth consecutive league win equalled the club record sequence from a season's start. The last occasion had been almost a century earlier in 1925-26.

4

For the first time ever the first four home league games were won to nil.

9

Nine wins from the opening 12 games equalled the club record at this stage, achieved on four previous occasions, most recently in 2021-22.

43

points were won at the SoL. This was the highest number at Championship level since the title was won under Roy Keane in 2006-07 when 49 were collected.

151

first team appearances were made by teenagers.

20

goals were scored by teenagers.

103

Chris Rigg's goal against Blackburn Rovers on Boxing Day was his seventh for the club. This saw him break Bobby Marshall's 103 year old record for the most goals scored by Sunderland by a player under the age of 18.

300

Luke O'Nien made his 300th appearance for Sunderland against Sheffield Wednesday in February. He became the first player to reach 300 appearances for the club since Michael Gray over 20 years ago.

155

O'Nien overtook John O'Shea's record of 138 appearances at the Stadium of Light. By the end of the season '09' had played 155 games at the stadium.

6

With three goals each, Trai Hume and Dennis Cirkin became the first full-back pairing to contribute six goals since 2012-13.

11

There were 11 first team debutants in 2024-25, the lowest number since 11 debuted in 2014-15.

34

Milan Aleksic was an unused sub on 34 occasions, surpassing Matt Kilgallon's record of being an unused sub 28 times in 2012-13.

THE WORLD TO SUNDERLAND

THE WOMEN'S RUGBY WORLD CUP AT THE SOL

The Women's Rugby World Cup is the top trophy in women's rugby. This summer the best 16 teams from all around the world competed in the tournament which was held in England for the first time since 2010. Eight venues were used for the competition with the Stadium of Light selected for the highly prestigious opening game. This saw England take on the USA in a repeat of the first two Women's Rugby World Cup finals of 1991 and 1994. The USA beat England 19-6 in 1991, but England won 38-23 four years later. In 2025 at Sunderland, the score was England 69-7 USA.

The United States joined Australia, Austria, Belgium, Scotland and Turkey in playing full internationals against England at the Stadium of Light. All of those other countries played at Sunderland in soccer rather than rugby internationals, with the Austria and Scotland internationals being women's games. As well as England and the USA, Australia, Brazil, Canada, Fiji, France, Ireland, Italy, Japan, New Zealand, Samoa, Scotland, Spain, South Africa and Wales all came together for the World Cup with the final staged at the home of rugby in Twickenham.

For the Stadium of Light to be the host of the Women's World Cup opening match was a big plus for Wearside. Screened worldwide, the high-profile tournament was a major moment in the sporting calendar with all eyes on Sunderland where a packed crowd of rugby fans from far and wide enjoyed the occasion at a top class venue.

Washington Old Hall

The USSR celebrate scoring against Italy at Sunderland in the 1966 FIFA World Cup © Alan Gibson

The All Blacks of 1924

STARS & STRIPES

The stripes on the USA flag are of course red and white so the American team should have felt at home at the Stadium of Light. American visitors to Sunderland for the big game had the opportunity to find out why Sunderland is so important to America. The first ever President of the USA was George Washington. The family of his ancestors lived at Washington Old Hall in Washington which is in Sunderland. George Washington's ancestors took their family name from the place where they lived. The original home of the first American President's relatives form part of what is a big tourist attraction. The oldest parts of the building date back to the 13th century. In the following century the family's coat of arms featured two stripes and three stars so perhaps the famous stars and stripes really has its origins in Sunderland. George Washington himself was born in America in the 1730s but his family history stems from Washington in Sunderland.

WORLD CUP WEARSIDE

Staging the first game of the 2025 Women's World Cup was a big achievement for SAFC but there have been World Cup matches in Sunderland before. This was in 1966 when England staged the football World Cup. Back then Sunderland's old ground Roker Park hosted four games including a quarter-final.

ROKER RUGBY

The England v USA match in the summer was the first ever rugby match played at the Stadium of Light, but Sunderland AFC have staged rugby matches before – albeit a very long time ago. Over a century ago in 1924 Sunderland's old ground Roker Park welcomed the New Zealand All Blacks who beat Durham County 43-7. In 1931 the South African Springboks defeated a combined Northumberland and Durham team 41-0. However, it is an even older former ground of SAFC that is the home of rugby on Wearside. Sunderland played at Ashbrooke's Grove Field in 1883. Grove Field was one of the fields purchased to set up 'Sunderland Cricket and Football Club' in 1887. Sunderland Rugby FC celebrated its 150th anniversary in the 2023-24 season and still plays at the beautiful Ashbrooke ground.

AFRICA CUP
OF NATIONS

The Africa Cup of Nations is one of the world's top international tournaments. It takes place in Morocco between 21 December 2025 and 18 January 2026. Who are the Sunderland players who could be called up for the tournament?

BERTRAND TRAORÉ – BURKINA FASO

At the time of his arrival at Sunderland, Bertrand had played 84 times for his country, scoring 22 goals. He has scored in three different African Cup of Nations finals tournaments, helping Burkina Faso to third place in the 2017 competition.

SIMON ADINGRA – IVORY COAST

Simon was the Player of the Match in the most recent AFCON final in 2023 when he provided both assists as his country beat Nigeria 2-1.

NOAH SADIKI & ARTHUR MASUAKU – DEMOCRATIC REPUBLIC OF CONGO

The DRC were semi-finalists in last year's AFCON tournament and have won the cup twice before. Noah Sadiki and Arthur Masuaku are likely to be important members of their squad. In the last tournament Masuaku scored in the quarter-final.

REINILDO – MOZAMBIQUE

Before joining Sunderland, Reinildo had made 49 appearances for Mozambique. Mozambique have never progressed beyond the group stage of AFCON. If that remains the case Reinildo might be available for Sunderland as soon as the Spurs game on 3 January.

CHEMSDINE TALBI – MOROCCO

Talbi was yet to win a cap for Morocco when he signed for Sunderland, but he had been in their squad earlier in 2025. Morocco won the tournament last in 1976, but they will hope being the host nation will help them to go deep into the competition.

2026 FIFA WORLD CUP

Under three weeks after the Premier League finishes on 24 May the FIFA World Cup takes place in Canada, Mexico and the USA between 11 June and 19 July 2026. All of Sunderland's international players will be hoping their countries qualify for that.

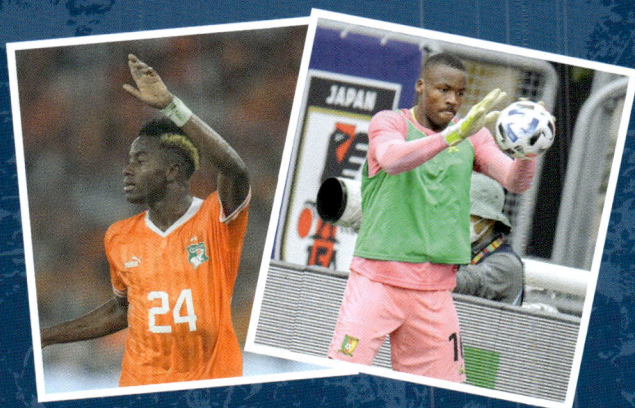

TOTAL ENERGIES: AFRICA CUP OF NATIONS

The Africa Cup of Nations features 24 countries. The games take place at nine different stadiums spread over six cities.

Sunderland players selected for the tournament might miss the games at Brighton and at home with Leeds United and Manchester City while the group stage takes place between 21 and 31 December.

The top two teams in each group and the best four third placed teams from the six groups will progress to the knock-out stages. The round of 16 takes place between 3 and 6 January with the quarter-finals on 9 and 10 January. Semi-finals are on 14 January with the third place game on 17 January. The final is a day later. Players who are away for the whole tournament will miss seven games including the FA Cup third round. The squad should be back to full strength for the trip to West Ham United on 24 January.

MATCHES TO LOOK OUT FOR

All 52 games of the tournament will be broadcast live by Sky Sports. Special matches to look forward to are listed below, where there might be a Sunderland player on each side.

24 December, Ivory Coast v Mozambique, Group F
This game could see Simon Adingra coming up against Reinildo. Adingra's Ivory Coast will be hot favourites to defeat Mozambique.

27 December, Senegal v DR Congo, Group D
Habib Diarra of Senegal could line-up against his SAFC teammates Noah Sadiki and Arthur Masuaku in this match which takes place at the Ibn Batouta Stadium in Tangier.

There could also be some key knockout games with Sunderland players on both sides.

50 PLUS

Mo Salah of Liverpool and Egypt, Amad of Manchester United and Ivory Coast, and Yves Bissouma of Spurs and Mali are among over 50 Premier League players who are expected to be at the tournament.

BLONDY NNA NOUKEU - CAMEROON

One of SAFC's back-up goalkeepers, Nna Noukeu has been in a Cameroon squad in the past but was uncapped at the start of the season and would be an outside bet for a place in the squad of five-time champions Cameroon.

AHMED ABDULLAHI – NIGERIA

Having played for Nigeria in the 2023 Under-20s, striker Abdullahi could force his way into his country's squad if he is doing well in the Premier League. Nigeria have been champions three times.

HABIB DIARRA – SENEGAL

Midfielder Diarra started this season with 11 caps for Senegal. Habib's four goals for his country include one against England in June. Senegal might win it again, as they did in 2021!

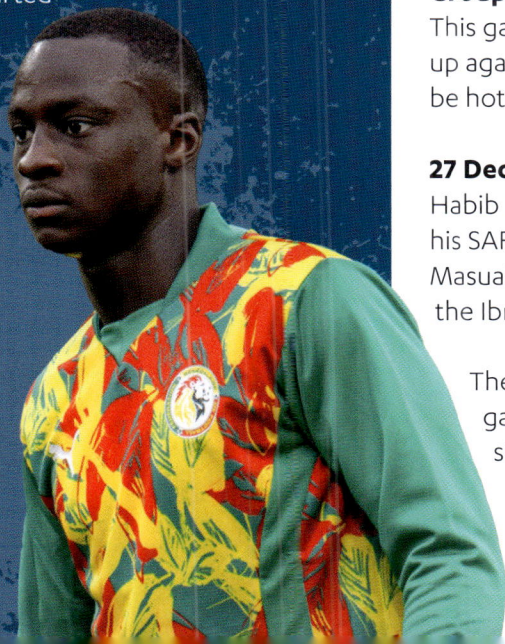

ON THE BALL

Can you work out which players are on the ball?

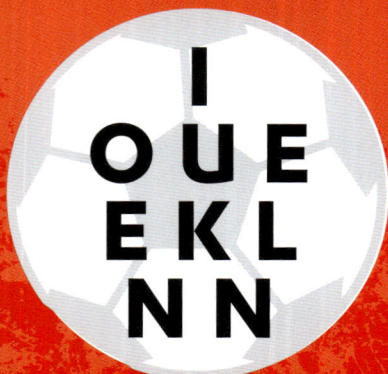

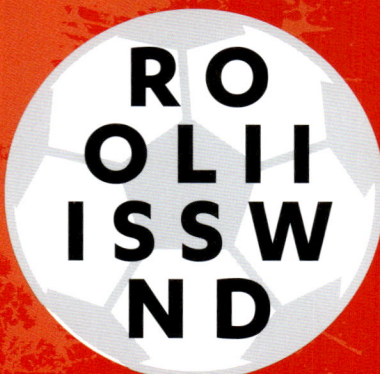

I O U E E K L N N

R O O L I I I S S W N D

M A A N E K S C I I L L

CORNERED

Can you guess which 4 players' faces make up the following image?

FACT OR FIB?

Which of these statements are facts – and which are fibs?

1) Northern Ireland international defender Dan Ballard was born in England.

2) Norway Under 21 international defender Leo Hjelde was born in England.

3) England Under 21 defender Dennis Cirkin was born in England.

SPOT THE SCORE-LINE

These four games finished in 4-0, 3-1, 3-2 and 2-0 wins for Sunderland last season. Can you connect the correct score to each game?

1) Sunderland – Sheffield Wednesday

2) Middlesbrough – Sunderland

3) Portsmouth – Sunderland

4) Sunderland – Luton Town

FIND THE ANSWERS ON PAGE 61.

12

DESIGN A KIT

NEW SIGNINGS

Following promotion to the Premier League Sunderland sensationally re-shaped their squad. Starting with confirming the transfer of Enzo Le Fée (who is featured on p 25) from Roma Sunderland went on to add another 13 signings.

(L) indicates a player was on loan to a club listed as one of their previous clubs but if a player then signed for the loan club the (L) is not used. For example, Reinildo Mandava was on loan at the French club Lille but then signed for them.

19

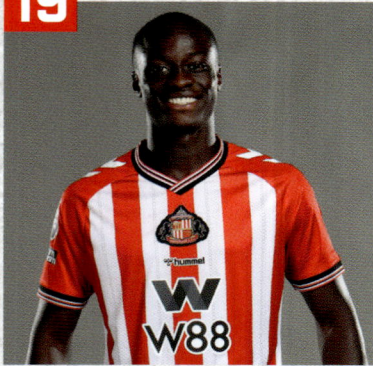

HABIB DIARRA

Birthplace: Guédiawaye, Senegal

Birthdate: 3 January 2004

Age at the start of the season: 21

Previous clubs: Mulhouse, Strasbourg

International: Senegal

2024-25 appearances: 27+3 for Strasbourg + 2 for Senegal

2024-25 goals: 4 for Strasbourg + 1 for Senegal

Midfielder Habib Diarra became Sunderland's record signing three weeks after scoring against England for Senegal in a summer friendly at Nottingham Forest's City Ground. He played just over 100 games in France for Strasbourg. Of these 94 were in Ligue 1 with the box-to-box player being used both offensively and defensively, as well as showing he could operate on either flank. Last season he skippered Strasbourg to seventh place in Ligue 1 as the club qualified for Europe with the midfielder contributing four goals and five assists. After playing youth football at Mulhouse, Diarra made his first team debut with Strasbourg in October 2021, coming off the bench late on in a 5-1 win against St. Etienne, for whom former Sunderland player Wahbi Khazri had scored. Raised in France where he moved as a boy, Habib represented France up to Under 21 level before becoming a full international for the country of his birth. His transfer fee to SAFC was officially undisclosed but was reported as being around £30m.

27

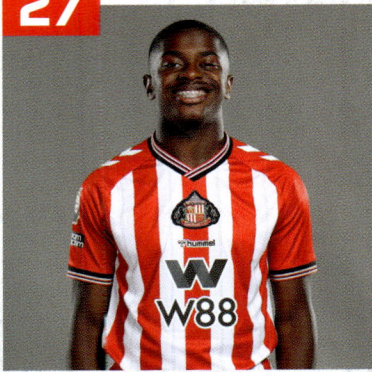

NOAH SADIKI

Birthplace: Brussels, Belgium

Birthdate: 17 December 2004

Age at the start of the season: 20

Previous clubs: RSC Anderlecht, Union Saint-Gilloise

International: DR Congo

2024-25 appearances: 49+2 for Union Saint-Gilloise plus 9 for DR Congo

2024-25 goals: 1 for Union Saint-Gillcise

An energetic midfielder who can also play in defence, Noah was a vital cog in the Union Saint-Gilloise machine that won the Belgian league last season. With close to 150 senior games and having tasted the Champions League, Europa League, Europa Conference League and international football Sadiki came to Sunderland with enormous experience for one so young. The 20-year-old won the Belgian Cup in 2024, coming off the bench as Antwerp were beaten in the final in a season where USG also went close to the league title. That summer Sadiki added the Belgian Super Cup to his honours when his side beat Club Brugge who had former Sunderland star Simon Mignolet in goal.

As a 6-year-old he began with RSC Anderlecht. Noah was 17 when Vincent Kompany handed him a debut against Mignolet and Club Brugge in May 2022. Noah's breakthrough season came the following year when 17 appearances included one at West Ham in the Europa Conference League, but that summer he moved on to USG.

Having been capped by Belgium at Under 16, 18, 19 and 20 level Sadiki decided to play for the country of his parents' birth, the Democratic Republic of Congo. After recognition at Under 21 level his full international debut came in September of 2024 against Guinea. The fee to buy him was undisclosed but widely reported a £15m with potentially another £2m in add-ons.

17

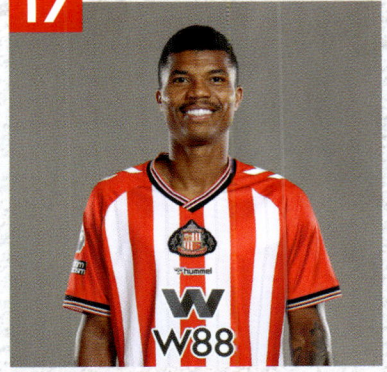

REINILDO

Birthplace: Beira, Mozambique

Birthdate: 21 January 1994

Age at the start of the season: 31

Previous clubs: Ferroviário de Beira, GD Maputo, Benfica B, Fafe (L), Sporting Covilhã (L), Belenenses SAD, Lille, Atlético Madrid

International: Mozambique

2024-25 appearances: 15+15 for Atlético Madrid plus 2 for Mozambique

2024-25 goals: 0

Known simply as Reinildo, the left back signed a two-year deal with Sunderland, arriving on a free transfer after leaving Atlético Madrid who he had just helped to third place in La Liga in Spain. During the season five of his appearances came in the Champions League. These included a victory away to Paris Saint-Germain, the same club he made his final Atlético appearance against in the Club World Cup in June. Previously, he had helped Lille to the Ligue 1 title in 2021. At the time of his move to Sunderland Reinildo had represented Mozambique 49 times, scoring four international goals.

7

CHEMSDINE TALBI

Birthplace: Sambreville, Belgium

Birthdate: 9 May 2005

Age at the start of the season: 20

Previous clubs: Tubize, Club NXT, Club Brugge

International: Belgium Under 18

2024-25 appearances: 19+19 for Club Brugge

2024-25 goals: 7 for Club Brugge

Having played for Belgium at Under 15, 17 and 18 level, scoring seven times in 20 games for the country of his birth, Chemsdine decided to represent Morocco. The winger was called up at senior level for the first time in March 2025, when he was still a teenager. Talbi will be hoping his form in the Premier League will earn him a place in the host nation's squad for the Africa Cup of Nations which takes place between 21 December and 18 January.

Winning the Belgian Cup with Brugge in 2025 climaxed a season in which Talbi's club finished a point behind champions Union St. Gilloise. Facing his new teammate Noah Sadiki in a clash between the top two, Chemsdine scored in a 2-2 draw. He also netted twice in an important Champions League win at Atalanta, one of 11 appearances he made in the Champions League last season. A teammate of former Sunderland goalkeeper Simon Mignolet at Brugge, Talbi was signed on a five-year contract. Officially the fee was undisclosed, but it was widely reported as £18m with a potential further £2.5m in add-ons.

24

SIMON ADINGRA

Birthplace: Abobo, Abidjan, Ivory Coast

Birthdate: 1 January 2002

Age at the start of the season: 23

Previous clubs: Right to Dream, Nordsjælland, Brighton & Hove Albion, Union Saint-Gilloise (L)

International: Ivory Coast

2024-25 appearances: 15+18 for Brighton

2024-25 goals: 5 for Brighton

An exciting player who can cause trouble on either wing, Simon was named the best young player at the last Africa Cup of Nations when he helped Ivory Coast to triumph in 2023. In that tournament Adingra was also named as Player of the Match in the final after he provided both assists as Nigeria were defeated 2-1 in the final. Simon will be hoping to help his country retain their crown this winter.

He joined Sunderland on a five-year deal for a fee reported to be £21m plus add-ons, although officially the amount remained undisclosed. Adingra first came to Europe to play in Denmark with Nordsjæland. Coming off the bench he made a debut impact with a last-minute goal against Copenhagen in April 2021. Having bagged another ten goals in just under 40 games – almost half of which were as a substitute – he was snapped up by Brighton after one full season and immediately loaned out to Belgian outfit Union Saint-Gilloise. There he played Champions League and Europa League football as his side missed out on their league title on goal difference, one of Simon's 11 goals being a winner away to the eventual champions.

Such form brought him back to Brighton where he marked his debut with a goal, as he had with his previous two clubs. He gained further Europa League experience with The Seagulls before joining SAFC, having netted a dozen times in two seasons playing for the south coast club.

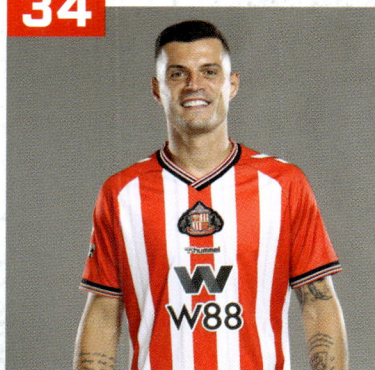

34

GRANIT XHAKA

Birthplace: Basel, Switzerland

Birthdate: 27 September 1992

Age at the start of the season: 32

Previous clubs: Concordia Basel, FC Basel, Borussia Mönchengladbach, Arsenal, Bayer Leverkusen

International: Switzerland

2024-25 appearances: 47+2 for Bayer Leverkusen plus 7 for Switzerland

2024-25 goals: 2 for Bayer Leverkusen

Named as the 16th best footballer in the world in the 2024 Ballon d'Or, Switzerland's captain and record appearance holder was a major summer signing for Sunderland. A commanding midfield powerhouse, Xhaka twice won the Swiss Super League as well as the Swiss Cup before moving to Borussia Mönchengladbach where he played over 100 times before moving to Arsenal in 2016 for £35m. He went on to captain The Gunners with whom he twice won the FA Cup. Renowned for scoring spectacular goals from long distance, one of his goals for Arsenal in 2021-22 was the club's Goal of the Season. With Bayer Leverkusen in 2023-24 he won the league, domestic cup (scoring the winner in the final) and German Supercup as well as playing in the Europa League final. Granit has made 32 appearances in the Champions League, 10 of them last season. He has played in the last three FIFA World Cups, scoring in two of those tournaments.

22

ROBIN ROEFS

Birthplace: Heeswijk, Netherlands

Birthdate: 17 January 2002

Age at the start of the season: 22

Previous clubs: VV Heeswijk, NEC Nijmegen

International: Netherlands Under 21

2024-25 appearances: 33 for NEC plus 5 for Netherlands Under 21s

2024-25 clean sheets: 10 for NEC plus 2 for Netherlands Under 21s

Goalkeeper Robin Roefs arrived at Sunderland from Dutch football for an undisclosed fee, but one that was reported as £11.5m. His ten league clean sheets last season had only once been bettered by Gábor Babos in NEC's history. In the top six European leagues last season only four goalkeepers statistically saved more goals than Roefs who was reckoned to have saved ten goals. Two of his clean sheets came away to two of his country's biggest clubs: Ajax and Feyenoord. Roefs' performances helped his club to eighth place and with it a Play-off place for European qualification. Robin also kept clean sheets in two of his five international Under 21 games last term.

26

ARTHUR MASUAKU

Birthplace: Lille, France

Birthdate: 7 November 1993

Age at the start of the season: 31

Previous clubs: Lille OSC Fives, Lens, Valenciennes, Olympiacos, West Ham United, Besiktas

International: DR Congo

2024-25 appearances: 40+2 for Besiktas plus 2 for DR Congo

2024-25 goals: 1 for Besiktas

An experienced player, Arthur made over 100 Premier League appearances for West Ham United between 2016 and 2022. With Besiktas he won the Turkish Cup and Super Cup in 2024 while in Greece he did the double with Olympiacos in 2015 and retained the league title a year later. Having played for France up to Under 19 level, Masuaku has been a full DR Congo international since 2018. He scored in the Europa League last season and has also netted in the Champions League, the Premier League and the Africa Cup of Nations. Last season he recorded a career high of ten assists.

15

OMAR ALDERETE

Birthplace: Asuncion, Paraguay

Birthdate: 26 December 1996

Age at the start of the season: 28

Previous clubs: Cerro Porteño, Gimnasia y Esgrima (L), Huracan, Basel, Hertha Berlin, Valencia (L), Getafe

International: Paraguay

2024-25 appearances: 35 for Getafe plus 9 for Paraguay

2024-25 goals: 1 for Getafe plus 2 for Paraguay

Scoring the winning goal for Paraguay in a victory over an Argentina side which included Lionel Messi was a highlight of last season for this experienced defender. A left-sided centre-back, Alderete was in the top 4% of centre-backs in Europe's top five leagues in terms of clearances last term. No stranger to scoring, Omar also has a powerful shot from long distance. Alderete has played club football in Paraguay, Argentina, Switzerland, Germany and Spain before coming to England. He also has experience of the Champions League and a goal to his name in that competition.

20

NORDI MUKIELE

Birthplace: Montreuil, France

Birthdate: 1 November 1997

Age at the start of the season: 27

Previous clubs: Paris FC, Laval, Montpellier, RB Leipzig, Paris Saint-Germain, Bayer Leverkusen (L)

International: France

2024-25 appearances: 19+5 for Bayer Leverkusen

2024-25 goals: 2 for Bayer Leverkusen

Capped by France in 2021, Nordi won silverware in Germany with RB Leipzig followed by five trophies with his home city club Paris Saint-Germain as well as gaining the experience of playing in over 30 Champions League games. These included the five last seasons as a teammate of Granit Xhaka at Bayer Leverkusen where one of Mukiele's goals was a Champions League winner against Inter Milan.

BRIAN BROBBEY

Birthplace: Amsterdam, Netherlands

Birthdate: 1 February 2002

Age at the start of the season: 23

Previous clubs: Ajax, RB Leipzig

International: Netherlands

2024-25 appearances: 31+11 for Ajax plus 2+1 for Netherlands

2024-25 goals: 7 for Ajax plus 1 for Netherlands

The Netherlands international arrived at Sunderland on transfer deadline day with 54 goals to his name from 168 games. Seventy of those games as a young player were as a substitute which makes Brain's goals to games ratio even better. After just a single league start for Ajax, along with a handful of appearances off the bench he was allowed to move on to RB Leipzig. There was also just one league start in Germany before Ajax brought him back. Ajax's Player of the Year in 2024, Brobbey has Champions League and Europa League experience.

6

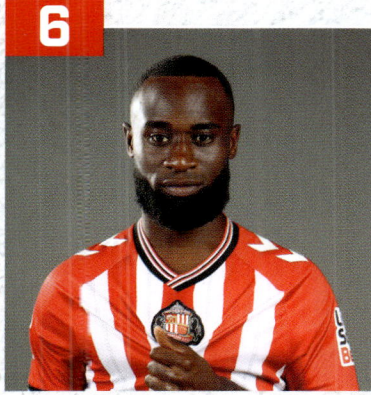

LUTSHAREL GEERTRUIDA

Birthplace: Rotterdam

Birthdate: 18 July 2000

Age at the start of the season: 25

Previous clubs: Feyenoord, RB Leipzig

International: Netherlands

2024-25 appearances: 3 for Feyenoord, 27+8 for RB Leipzig, plus 2 +4 for Netherlands.

2024-25 goals: 1 for RB Leipzig

Signed on an initial season long loan from RB Leipzig, Geertruida won the league and cup in his homeland with Feyenoord for whom he also played in the 2022 Europa Conference League final as well as being selected for that tournament's Team of the Season. Able to play in defence or as a defensive midfielder, in the 2023 European Nations semi-final and at Euro 2024.

BERTRAND TRAORÉ

Birthplace: Bobo-Dioulasso, Burkina Faso

Birthdate: 6 September 1995

Age at the start of the season: 29

Previous clubs: Chelsea, Vitesse Arnhem (L), Lyon, Aston Villa, Basaksehir, Villareal, Ajax

International: Burkina Faso

2024-25 appearances: 28+19 for Ajax plus 1+2 for Burkina Faso

2024-25 goals: 10 for Ajax plus 1 for Burkina Faso

A full international since the age of 15, Bertrand has a wealth of experience in all European competitions as well as playing for clubs in the Netherlands, France, Turkey, Spain and England. With Chelsea he scored in a 5-1 Premier League win over Newcastle United while during his time with Aston Villa Traoré was involved in a stunning 7-2 victory over Liverpool.

PLAYER PROFILES

1

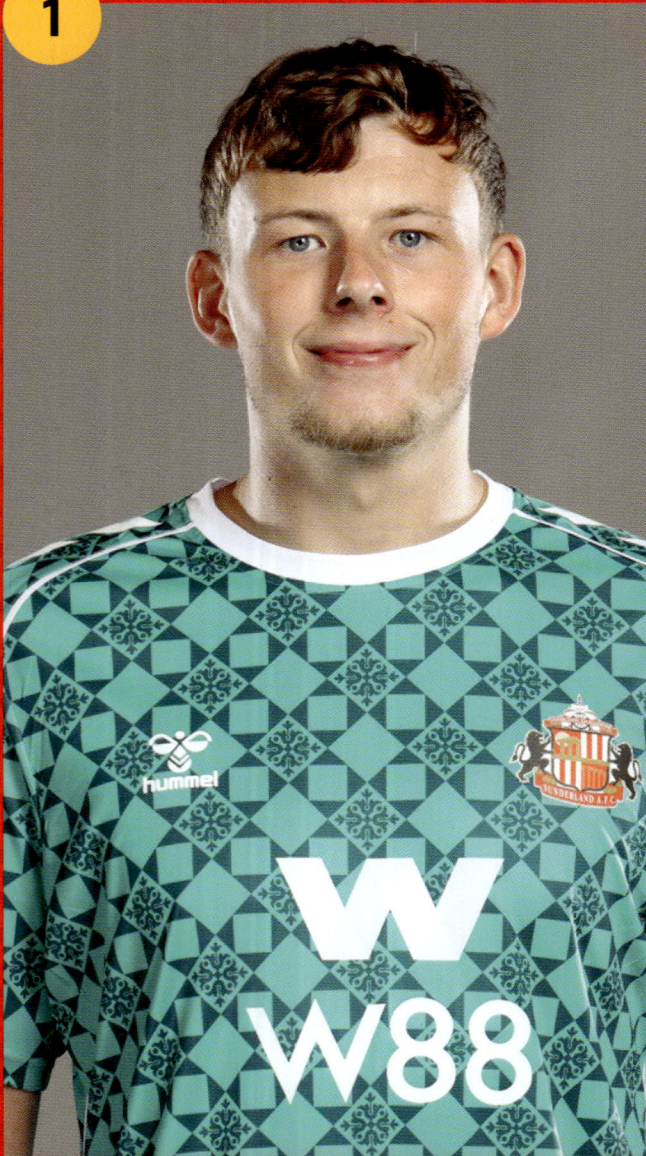

ANTHONY PATTERSON
GOALKEEPER

'Patto' earned his place in Sunderland folklore with two crucial saves in last year's Play-off final. As much as anyone Anthony played a vital role in getting SAFC into the Premier League. His second minute save to deny Keiffer Moore's header was a classically brilliant full length save as Patterson clawed the ball away. His later stop from Andre Brooks was more unorthodox with his feet but it was just as important, not least as Sunderland equalised six minutes later and went on to win. Anthony has been with the club since he was nine and in 2022 he was the North East Football Writers' Player of the Year.

Birthplace: Newcastle

Birthdate: 10 May 2000

Age at the start of the season: 25

Previous clubs: None

Clubs loaned to by Sunderland: Sunderland RCA, Notts County

International: England Under 21

2024-25 appearances: 45

2024-25 clean sheets: 14

SIMON MOORE

GOALKEEPER

Simon began this season needing six appearances to reach a career total of 300. His brother Stuart is a goalkeeper for Wycombe Wanderers.

Birthplace: Sandown, Isle of Wight

Birthdate: 19 May 1990

Age at the start of the season: 35

Previous clubs: Brading Town, Southampton, Farnborough, Brentford, Basingstoke Town (L), Cardiff City, Bristol City (L), Sheffield United, Coventry City

International: Isle of Wight

2024-25 appearances: 6

2024-25 clean sheets: 3

MATTY YOUNG

GOALKEEPER

A very highly rated keeper who kept six clean sheets in a row for Salford and won the Young Player of the Year award when on loan with Darlington. Matty is spending this season on loan to Salford City again.

Birthplace: Durham

Birthdate: 24 November 2006

Age at the start of the season: 18

Previous clubs: None

Clubs loaned to by Sunderland: Darlington, Salford City

International: England Under 20

2024-25 appearances: 27 (For Salford)

2024-25 clean sheets: 9 (for Salford)

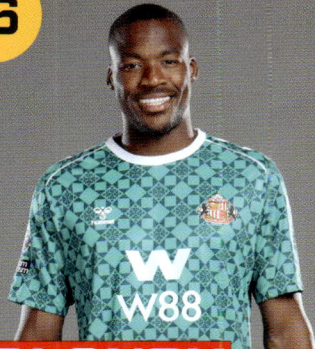

BLONDY NNA NOUKEU

GOALKEEPER

Blondy's dad Patrice was a midfielder who played in Belgium, Greece and Azerbaijan. In May of 2025 he became manager of Canon Yaoundé in the top division in Cameroon.

Birthplace: Doula, Cameroon

Birthdate: 17 September 2001

Age at the start of the season: 23

Previous clubs: Royal Excel Mouscron, Stoke City, Crawley Town (L), Southend Utd (L)

International: Cameroon Under 21

2024-25 appearances: 0

2024-25 clean sheets: 0

32

TRAI HUME
DEFENDER

Sunderland's Player of the Year and Players' Player of the Year, 'Huuuuuume's' consistency and determination were key factors in the side's success.

Birthplace: Ballymena, Northern Ireland

Birthdate: 18 March 2002

Age at the start of the season: 23

Previous clubs: Linfield, Ballymena United (L)

Clubs loaned to by Sunderland: None

International: Northern Ireland

2024-25 appearances: 47+1

2024-25 goals: 3

3

DENNIS CIRKIN
DEFENDER

A quality defender who is a serious goal threat when he gets forward.

Birthplace: Dublin, Republic of Ireland

Birthdate: 6 April 2002

Age at the start of the season: 23

Previous clubs: Ridgeway Rovers, Tottenham Hotspur

Clubs loaned to by Sunderland: None

International: England Under 20

2024-25 appearances: 33+6

2024-25 goals: 3

5

DAN BALLARD
DEFENDER

Ballard was a major factor in getting Sunderland into the Premier League. Just back from injury, he was defiant in the face of pressure in both legs of the Play-off semi-final. Dan then scored the very late winner before being excellent again in the final.

Birthplace: Stevenage

Birthdate: 22 September 1999

Age at the start of the season: 25

Previous clubs: Arsenal, Swindon Town (L), Blackpool (L), Millwall (L)

Clubs loaned to by Sunderland: None

International: Northern Ireland

2024-25 appearances: 15+8

2024-25 goals: 3

13

LUKE O'NIEN
DEFENDER

Unlucky to be injured in the opening minutes of the Play-off final, O'Nien's experience and leadership qualities as club captain were a big help in the promotion season.

Birthplace: Hemel Hempstead

Birthdate: 21 November 1994

Age at the start of the season: 30

Previous clubs: Watford, Wealdstone (L), Wycombe Wanderers

Clubs loaned to by Sunderland: None

International: None

2024-25 appearances: 48+1

2024-25 goals: 3

42

AJI ALESE
DEFENDER

Outstanding when he played, unfortunately Aji missed much of last season through injury. He will hope to be more involved this season.

Birthplace: Islington

Birthdate: 17 January 2001

Age at the start of the season: 24

Previous clubs: West Ham United, Accrington Stanley (L), Cambridge United (L)

Clubs loaned to by Sunderland: None

International: England Under 20

2024-25 appearances: 9+4

2024-25 goals: 0

33

LEO HJELDE
DEFENDER

Always dependable, Leo was often used as a late sub to shore up a positive result in the promotion campaign.

Birthplace: Nottingham

Birthdate: 26 August 2003

Age at the start of the season: 21

Previous clubs: Celtic, Ross County (L), Leeds United, Rotherham United (L)

Clubs loaned to by Sunderland: None

International: Norway Under 21

2024-25 appearances: 7+12

2024-25 goals: 0

23

JENSON SEELT
DEFENDER

Jenson is on loan to Bundesliga outfit VfL Wolfsburg for the 2025-26 season.

Birthplace: Ede, Netherlands

Birthdate: 23 May 2003

Age at the start of the season: 22

Previous clubs: PSV Eindhoven

Clubs loaned to by Sunderland: None

International: None

2024-25 appearances: 0+1

2024-25 goals: 0

2

NIALL HUGGINS
DEFENDER

Missed all of last season through injury so Niall will hope for full fitness and regular football this time round. Niall is on loan to Wycombe Wanderers during 2025-26.

Birthplace: York

Birthdate: 18 December 2000

Age at the start of the season: 24

Previous clubs: Heworth, Leeds United

Clubs loaned to by Sunderland: None

International: Wales Under 21

2024-25 appearances: 0

2024-25 goals: 0

41

ZAK JOHNSON
DEFENDER

Birthplace: Sunderland

Birthdate: 30 July 2004

Age at the start of the season: 21

Previous clubs: None

Clubs loaned to by Sunderland: Hartlepool United, Dundalk, Notts County

International: England Under 18

2024-25 appearances: 1 plus 5+5 for Notts County

2024-25 goals: 0

28

ENZO LE FÉE
MIDFIELDER

Had a hand in four of Sunderland's five Play-off goals and then became the club's record signing when his loan from Roma became a transfer for a reported £19m. Le Fée's final game for Roma saw him come up against former Sunderland hero, Fabio Borini of Sampdoria.

Birthplace: Lorient, France

Birthdate: 3 February 2000

Age at the start of the season: 25

Previous clubs: Lorient, Rennes, Roma

Clubs loaned to by Sunderland: None

International: France Under 21

2024-25 appearances: 14+4 plus 6+4 for Roma

2024-25 goals: 1

4

DAN NEIL
MIDFIELDER

Captained the side to promotion having played almost every game as the main midfield anchor.

Birthplace: South Shields

Birthdate: 13 December 2001

Age at the start of the season: 23

Previous clubs: None

Clubs loaned to by Sunderland: None

International: England Under 20

2024-25 appearances: 48

2024-25 goals: 2

11

CHRIS RIGG
MIDFIELDER

Still 17 when the season ended, Chris has done magnificently so far and seems set to have a stellar career.

Birthplace: Hebburn

Birthdate: 18 June 2007

Age at the start of the season: 18

Previous clubs: None

Clubs loaned to by Sunderland: None

International: England Under 19

2024-25 appearances: 39+8

2024-25 goals: 4

10

PATRICK ROBERTS

MIDFIELDER

The master of nutmegging defenders, his seven assists last season were more than anyone else, including his pass to Eliezer Mayenda at Wembley. Patrick has joined Birmingham City on loan for the 2025-26 campaign.

Birthplace: Kingston upon Thames

Birthdate: 5 February 1997

Age at the start of the season: 28

Previous clubs: Molesey Juniors, AFC Wimbledon, Fulham, Manchester City, Celtic (L), Girona (L), Norwich City (L), Middlesbrough (L), Derby County (L), Troyes (L)

Clubs loaned to by Sunderland: None

International: England Under 20

2024-25 appearances: 40+8

2024-25 goals: 2

30

MILAN ALEKSIĆ

MIDFIELDER

Having had a year to settle into English football the Serbian will hope to push on this season.

Birthplace: Kragujevac, Serbia

Birthdate: 30 August 2005

Age at the start of the season: 19

Previous clubs: FK Radniči 1923

Clubs loaned to by Sunderland: None

International: Serbia Under 21

2024-25 appearances: 3+6

2024-25 goals: 1

8

ALAN BROWNE

MIDFIELDER

A very experienced player who lost his place early in the season through injury but never let the team down when called upon. Alan is spending 2025-26 on loan to Middlesbrough.

Birthplace: Cork, Republic of Ireland

Birthdate: 15 April 1995

Age at the start of the season: 30

Previous clubs: Cork City, Preston North End

Clubs loaned to by Sunderland: None

International: Republic of Ireland

2024-25 appearances: 13+10

2024-25 goals: 1

50

HARRISON JONES

MIDFIELDER

Last season was the local lad's breakthrough season. Frequently on the bench, he impressed whenever given an opportunity.

Birthplace: York

Birthdate: 25 December 2004

Age at the start of the season: 20

Previous clubs: None

Clubs loaned to by Sunderland: None

International: None

2024-25 appearances: 3+3

2024-25 goals: 0

ADIL AOUCHICHE

MIDFIELDER

Spent the second half of last season impressing on loan at Portsmouth. Aouchiche is spending this season on loan to Aberdeen.

Birthplace: Le Blanc-Mesnil, France

Birthdate: 15 July 2002

Age at the start of the season: 23

Previous clubs: Mitry Mory, Tremblay, Paris Saint-Germain, St. Etienne, Lorient

Clubs loaned to by Sunderland: Portsmouth

International: France Under 20

2024-25 appearances: 5+5 plus 9+3 on loan to Portsmouth

2024-25 goals: 0 plus 1 on loan to Portsmouth

12

ELIEZER MAYENDA

FORWARD

'Hey Big Man – What's Your Name?' as the Mayenda chant starts. Being the scorer of two great goals in the Play-offs as well as the Goal of the Season has made Mayenda a hero.

Birthplace: Zaragoza, Spain

Birthdate: 8 May 2005

Age at the start of the season: 20

Previous clubs: Ebro, Breuillet, CS Brétigny and Sochaux

Clubs loaned to by Sunderland: Hibernian

International: Spain Under 21

2024-25 appearances: 26+15

2024-25 goals: 10

18

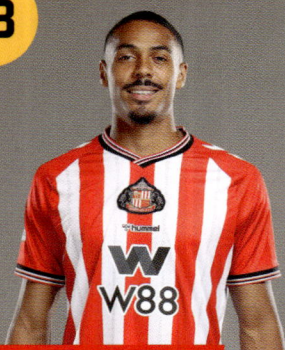

WILSON ISIDOR
FORWARD

Top scorer last season with three of his 13 goals nominated for the Goal of the Season award.

Birthplace: Rennes, France

Birthdate: 27 August 2000

Age at the start of the season: 24

Previous clubs: Rennes, Monaco, Laval (L), Bastia-Borgo (L), Lokomotiv Moscow and Zenit St. Petersburg

Clubs loaned to by Sunderland: None

International: France Under 20

2024-25 appearances: 36+10 plus 0+3 for Zenit

2024-25 goals: 13 Plus 1 for Zenit

11

ROMAINE MUNDLE
FORWARD

An exciting attacking threat on the left flank, Romaine returned from injury to help Sunderland win the Play-offs.

Birthplace: Edmonton, London

Birthdate: 24 April 2003

Age at the start of the season: 22

Previous clubs: Tottenham Hotspur, Standard Liege

Clubs loaned to by Sunderland: None

International: None

2024-25 appearances: 19+6

2024-25 goals: 5

47

TREY OGUNSUYI
FORWARD

A very bright teenage striker who scored 15 goals in 17+2 Under 21 games and 7 in 6 Under 18 outings last season when he made his first team debut in the FA Cup. Ogunsuyi is spending the 2025-26 season on loan to Falkirk.

Birthplace: Bradford

Birthdate: 26 November 2006

Age at the start of the season: 18

Previous clubs: None

Clubs loaned to by Sunderland: None

International: Belgium Under 19

2024-25 appearances: 0+1

2024-25 goals: 0

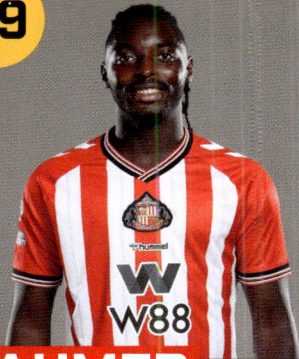

AHMED ABDULLAHI
FORWARD

Out injured for most of his first season at Sunderland, on his occasional appearances for the Under 21s Ahmed looked highly promising – like a new Kenwyne Jones.

Birthplace: Nasarawa, Nigeria

Birthdate: 19 June 2004

Age at the start of the season: 21

Previous clubs: Gent

Clubs loaned to by Sunderland: None

International: Nigeria Under 20

2024-25 appearances: 0

2024-25 goals: 0

LUÍS SEMEDO
FORWARD

After spending last season on loan in Italy, 'Hemir' is on loan to Moreirense in Portugal in 2025-26.

Birthplace: Lisbon, Portugal

Birthdate: 11 August 2003

Age at the start of the season: 22

Previous clubs: Benfica

Clubs loaned to by Sunderland: Juventus Next Gen

International: Portugal Under 20

2024-25 appearances: 0+1 plus, 29 for Juventus Next Gen

2024-25 goals: 0 plus, 3 for Juventus Next Gen

GRANIT
XHAKA

DAN
BALLARD

SPOT THE STADIUM

Can you tell which Premier League stadiums are pictured below?

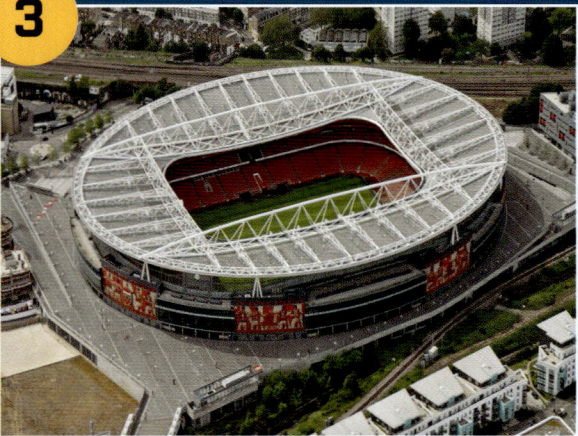

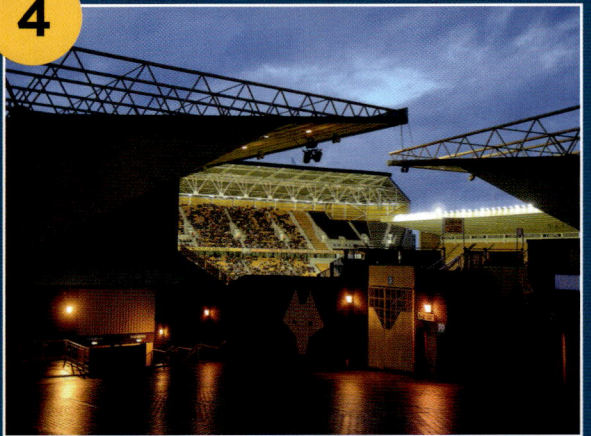

WHO IS IT?

Can you work out who the following four players are from the clues?

1) I signed for Sunderland in July 2022.

2) My previous club was West Ham United.

3) At the time I signed for Sunderland I had 23 caps for England at various levels up to Under 20.

4) Before coming to Sunderland I had been on loan to Cambridge United and Accrington Stanley.

5) I played for Sunderland against Luton Town in the 2023 Play-offs but then missed a long spell because of injury.

1 _____

1) I signed for Sunderland in June 2022.

2) My previous club was Arsenal.

3) I am a Northern Ireland international.

4) Before coming to Sunderland I had been on loan to Swindon Town, Blackpool and Millwall.

5) Although I am a defender, last season I scored in consecutive wins against Swansea City and Norwich City.

2 _____

1) I signed for Sunderland in July 2023.

2) My previous club was Sochaux in France.

3) I have played for Spain at Under 21 level.

4) After joining Sunderland I went on loan to Hibs in Scotland.

5) Last season I scored four goals against Sheffield Wednesday.

3 _____

1) I originally joined Sunderland on loan in August 2024.

2) My previous club was Zenit St. Petersburg in Russia.

3) Before signing for Sunderland I had played 23 times for France up to Under 20 level.

4) I played against Kylian Mbappe and Neymar on my league debut for Monaco against PSG in 2018 when I was 18.

5) Last season I was Sunderland's top scorer.

4 _____

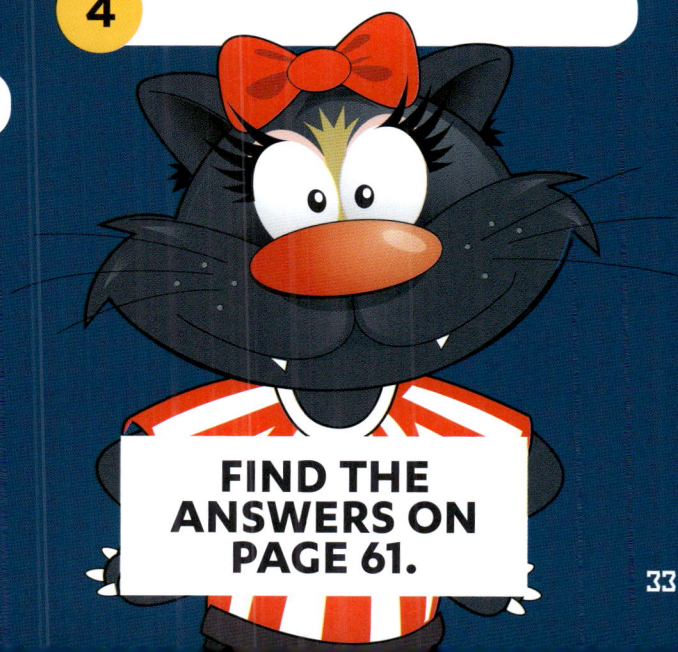

FIND THE ANSWERS ON PAGE 61.

'TIL THE END
SEASON REVIEW

The 2024/25 season proved to be one of the most exciting and successful in Sunderland's recent history. The previous season had seen Sunderland finish 16th after ending the campaign with ten defeats and just two wins from the last 15 games. The summer had seen the largely unknown Régis Le Bris appointed as head coach having never previously worked in English football. Before the end of the summer transfer window Le Bris lost the reigning Player of the Year Jack Clarke, and yet the Frenchman brilliantly managed to get the Lads back into the Premier League after eight years out of the top-flight.

BEST START

Opening with a first day win at Cardiff City, Régis le Bris joined Denis Smith, Steve Bruce and Roy Keane to become the fourth SAFC gaffer to begin their stint with an away win. There was even better to come as the team went on to win their first three league games without conceding a goal for the first time ever in their 134 years as a league club. A fourth consecutive league win equalled the club record sequence from a season's start.

The last occasion had been almost a century earlier in 1925/26 when, for the first time ever, the first four home league games were won without a goal being conceded. These four clean sheets from the first four home games represented the third best run of home clean sheets at the start of the season in Sunderland's history.

Only in 1899/1900 and 2021/21 when five had been chalked up had this been bettered.

It wasn't just the first few games that provided the base for the promotion campaign. The great start continued. After 13 fixtures Sunderland had picked up 29 points.

The only seasons Sunderland enjoyed a better start than last season were way back in the century before last. In 1894/95, the equivalent of 32 points were taken from the opening 13 games. In 1892/93 the equivalent of 31 points were acquired in the first 13 league matches. In both seasons Sunderland became league Champions.

Before 1981/82 it was two points for a win, but these comparisons are based on the number of points that would have been won had it always been three for a win.

BEST STARTS

The best starts after 13 league games:

1894/95 tier 1	10 wins	32 points
1892/93 tier 1	10 wins	31 points
2024/25 tier 2	9 wins	29 points
1899/00 tier 1	9 wins	28 points
1921/22 tier 1	9 wins	28 points
1925/26 tier 1	9 wins	28 points
1955/56 tier 1	9 wins	28 points
2021/22 tier 3	9 wins	28 points

YOUNGEST TEAM

Sunderland regularly fielded the youngest team not only in the Championship but in the entire Football League and Premier League. Le Bris's babes were the youngest team to ever win a Championship Play-off final. The line-up at Wembley had an average age of 24.3 years. It was not an inexperienced side though, as the players already had over 1,700 appearances under their belts. Throughout the season SAFC actually fielded even younger sides on a regular basis, with the youngest starting XI being just 22.4 years for a home game with Bristol City. That team included 17-year-old Chris Rigg and fellow teenagers Jobe, Tommy Watson and Eliezer Mayenda, with only 27-year-old on loan defender Chris Mepham being over 25. Over the course of the 46 game league campaign, Sunderland's average age was 23 years and 324 days.

Chris Rigg totalled 3,120 minutes of league action, more than any player at any club since Ryan Sessegnon of Fulham in 2017/18. Jobe played 3,717 minutes which is more than any teenager in the last decade.

FRENCH CONNECTION

When Régis Le Bris was installed as Sunderland's head coach the existing French connection at SAFC seemed to be set to play an influential role. That's not how things turned out as Pierre Ekwah, Timothée Pembélé, Abdoullah Ba and Adil Aouchiche were all sent out on loan. Nonetheless there was still to be a major French impression at Sunderland as Wilson Isidor and Enzo Le Fée were initially recruited on loan before their moves were made permanent after both played an important part in the promotion success.

'TIL THE END

In the run up to the Play-offs Sunderland created a campaign called 'Til The End'. This saw the front entrance of the stadium, the team bus and various places around the city covered in pictures of a fierce looking black cat with claws and teeth bared. When the teams emerged from the tunnel for the second leg of the crucial game with Coventry City a gigantic tifo of a demonic black cat was raised behind the Roker End goal. All this built an astonishing atmosphere as thousands of fans began match night by lining the streets to welcome the arrival of the team to the SoL and then cranked up the noise when the players came out onto the pitch. Once the game got going the noise was incredible as the team worked together – the team being the players and the crowd, "It was really impressive. The atmosphere was crazy" said head coach Régis Le Bris. "They helped a lot because we went through difficult moments, their energy was contagious. They were our twelfth man, really. I think it makes the difference."

BALLARD'S MOMENT

"I was just so determined. I got up too early. I was so determined. I can't remember what happened. It just happened like that, aww, it's some feeling." This was Dan Ballard's excited reaction barely a couple of minutes after his goal in the dying seconds of the Play-off semi-final as he spoke to Sky Sports while he was still on the pitch. Having just come back from injury with a half hour on the last day of the regular season against QPR, Ballard had been majestic in both legs of the Play-off semi-final with Coventry City. The Northern Ireland international constantly headed balls out of the penalty area in all 210 minutes of the semi-final and then climaxed his good work with a header in the opposition box with seconds left of the added time in extra time. It was the most dramatic final minute in the Stadium of Light's history and one that wrote Dan Ballard's name firmly into SAFC folklore. "It was fantastic. That late winner – what a moment" commented Régis Le Bris. "For the fans, and for everyone who loves Sunderland, it was probably the most powerful way to experience it right to the end."

The view of the Sunderland end at Wembley as seen from Sheffield United's end.

WEMBLEY

Wearside descended on London. On the night before the Play-off final against Sheffield United there wasn't a Blades supporter to be seen as SAFC's red and white army took over Trafalgar Square and Covent Garden. Tens of thousands of Sunderland supporters met there to sing songs, fly flags and in some cases to have a plodge in the fountains as the fans limbered up for the big event at Wembley the following day.

At the National Stadium the Lads took on the men from Bramall Lane. The Blades had been a highly efficient side throughout the season and had won as many points as it normally takes to be promoted automatically. They were favourites to go up but held no fears for the Black Cats. Sunderland had been desperately unlucky to lose at Bramall Lane during the season and had beaten the Blades at the Stadium of Light. Whereas

Sunderland had managed to get some extra tickets for the final as demand was so high, the Sheffield club had not managed to sell out their allocation. United still had a very big following for the final but there was never any doubt that it would be Sunderland fans who would be the noisiest. As the teams came out the Sunderland end was filled with a giant tifo and a spectacular red and white display, while at the opposite end the scarves that were twirled above heads paled into insignificance in comparison.

That support was needed when Sheffield United had the better of the first part of the game. In the opening couple of minutes Anthony Patterson had to make an incredible save in an incident that saw Sunderland centre-back Luke O'Nien dislocate his shoulder and have to be replaced. United then went ahead with a breakaway goal by Tyrese Campbell mid-way through the first half. Ten minutes later it looked like the Lads had gone

two down when Harrison Burrows blasted home from the edge of the box from Sheffield United's only corner of the game. Fortunately, VAR came to Sunderland's rescue. It was judged that Blades man Vini Souza had impeded Patterson's ability to see and dive for the ball, and with Sheffield United's Brazilian midfielder in an offside position the "goal" was disallowed.

Sunderland started to grow into the game shortly before half-time. After the break they were revitalised and pushed forward with more and more purpose. However they still needed Patterson to make another great save. The keeper used his feet to deny Andre Brooks in the 70th minute – the same minute that Jim Montgomery had produced his legendary save in the FA Cup final in 1973. That 1973 omen came into play moments later when Brighton bound Tommy Watson came off the bench in the 73rd minute.

Three minutes later Sunderland were deservedly level when Watson found Enzo Le Fée. The Frenchman's astute pass played in Watson's fellow sub Patrick Roberts who fed the ball through to Eliezer Mayenda. The Spain Under 21 international brilliantly crashed the ball into the roof of the net. Absolute bedlam greeted Wembley, "Has Wembley Stadium ever heard or felt noise and vibrations like that?!" asked BBC Sport's Ben Ashton as Sunderland took over, completely dominating the latter stages.

After winning the Play-off semi-final with late goals in both legs, Mayenda's at Coventry and Ballard's "couldn't be later" header at the SoL

there were just a couple of minutes to go when Tommy Watson collected a loose ball in midfield. Watson had already agreed to be transferred to Brighton and Hove Albion. These were to be the former Easington Academy pupil's last couple of minutes in the shirt of the club he had been with since he was six. As he had done so often in his years in the academy, Tommy took the ball towards the opponent's goal with one aim in mind. He didn't look to play in a teammate or blast the ball goal-wards. Instead, the 19-year-old placed a shot with deadly accuracy low into the corner of the net from outside the penalty area, cleverly curling his shot around a defender who obscured the view of his goalkeeper.

As the ball nestled in the back of the net Wembley and Wearside exploded. There was no time for Sheffield to come back. The Blades' century long wait for a Wembley win would be extended further. For Sunderland it was a third Wembley triumph in a row and the first time Sunderland had come from behind to win at the national stadium since the club's first ever trip there for the 1937 FA Cup final.

The celebrations went long into the night and beyond, with no Sunderland supporters leaving Wembley for a good hour or more as the players danced, celebrated and sprayed each other with champagne. Having never previously been away from the top level of English football for longer than six seasons, victory in the Play-off final brought an end to eight long years out of the Premier League as Sunderland's young side returned to the top in the most exciting and exhilarating fashion.

END OF SEASON
AWARDS

SAFC's End of Season Awards was a glamourous evening held at the Beacon of Light on the night after the final game of the regular season, but before the Play-offs. The women's team had completed their fixtures on the afternoon of the dinner, but everyone was super smart by the time SAFSEE commentator Frankie Francis hosted a sparkling show.

MEN

PLAYER AND PLAYERS' PLAYER OF THE SEASON

Trai Hume's season of consistent excellence saw the Northern Ireland international full back carry off two awards. Huuuuuuuume barely missed a game during the season, chipped in with a couple of winning goals and was defensively solid and determined throughout the campaign. Wilson Isidor, Jobe, Dan Neil, Chris Mepham and Luke O'Nien were all short-listed for the Player of the Season vote while midfielders Jobe and Dan Neil were also nominated for the Players' Player award.

YOUNG PLAYER
OF THE SEASON

Chris Rigg, Eliezer Mayenda and Romaine Mundle were all nominated for this award which went to Jobe who had already won the Sky Bet Championship Young Player of the Season award at the EFL awards night in London. At that same EFL dinner Chris Rigg had won the Sky Bet Championship Apprentice of the Season award.

WOMEN

PLAYERS' PLAYER
OF THE SEASON

Full time firefighter Megan Beer scooped this award from her teammates as she announced her retirement after 12 years as a member of the first team squad. Katie Kitching and Natasha Fenton had also been nominated.

WOMEN

PLAYER OF THE SEASON

Nominated for this award in both of her seasons since joining from London City Lionesses, New Zealand international Katie Kitching took the honour from a short-list that included Emily Dale, Amy Goddard, Mary McAteer, 2024 winner Emily Scarr and Libbi McInnes.

WOMEN

YOUNG PLAYER
OF THE SEASON

Midfielder Libbi McInnes took this award after a season in which she featured in over 20 games and was also nominated for the senior award. 2024 winner Mary McAteer, Mary Corbyn and Jessie Stapleton all reached the short-list for the Young Player of the Season accolade.

COMMUNITY PLAYER OF THE SEASON

Club captain Luke O'Nien is the squad's Professional Footballers' Association Community Champion. An outstanding role model, Luke is always a big supporter of the valuable work of the Foundation of Light.

JUNIOR PLAYER OF THE SEASON

Just as the Professional Development Phase Players of the Season were brothers, the Junior Player of the Season also has a brother at the club. Under 13s player Liam Ogunsuyi won this award in a season when his performances had seen him involved with the Under 15 and Under 16 sides as well as his own age group. Older brother Trey also had a great season, scoring regularly for the Under-21s and making his first-team debut.

PROFESSIONAL DEVELOPMENT PHASE PLAYERS OF THE SEASON

There were awards for both the Under 18 and Under 21 age groups – and both went to the same family with brothers Jayden and Harrison Jones scooping the prizes. Both players have been with the club since they were six-year-olds so these awards were the result of a lot of hard work. During the season, Under 21 captain Harrison had begun to break through into the first team while Jayden had made a similar step up, increasingly playing for the Under 21s rather than the Under 18s.

LIFETIME ACHIEVEMENT AWARD

Academy coach Carlton Fairweather worked at SAFC for well over 20 years. Once a top-flight player with Wimbledon, Carlton started at Sunderland in 2003. Between then and 2025 the Londoner helped many players to develop from youngsters into first teamers. This was the case for both the men's and women's teams. For three years Carlton managed the women's team. Until midway through the 2024/25 season he was one of the coaches of the men's Under 18 side. Sadly Carlton became very ill during the season and passed away in April. His widow Lesley received the award for Carlton who was one of the most popular people at the club, as he was such a warm and friendly person who always had time and a big smile for everyone.

WOMEN'S GOAL OF THE SEASON

There were six nominations for the Women's Goal of the Season, two each from the dynamic Katie Kitching and lethal Eleanor Dale, with one each from Libbi McInnes and Natasha Fenton. McInnes made it a personal double for the evening, having her goal voted the winner to go with her award as Young Player of the Year.

KATIE KITCHING
VS CHARLTON ATHLETIC [A]

A brilliant free-kick from the right side whipped into the top corner.

ELEANOR DALE
VS EXETER CITY [A]

Eleanor outmuscled her marker and drove down the left wing, before unleashing a powerful left-footed strike, the first of four she scored in this game.

KATIE KITCHING
VS BRISTOL CITY [H]

The league's November Goal of the Month nomination.

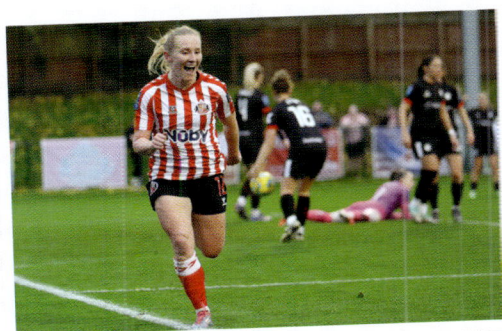

NATASHA FENTON
VS CHARLTON ATHLETIC [H]

An excellent free-kick, which won the league's March Goal of the Month award.

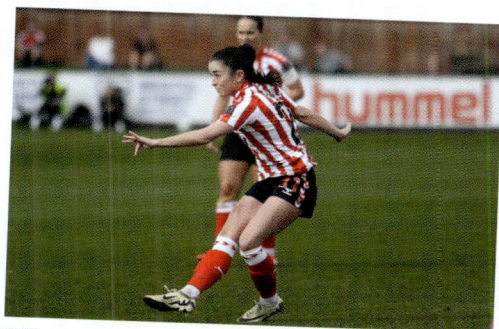

ELEANOR DALE
VS SOUTHAMPTON [A]

Received a Barclays Women's Championship January Goal of the Month nomination.

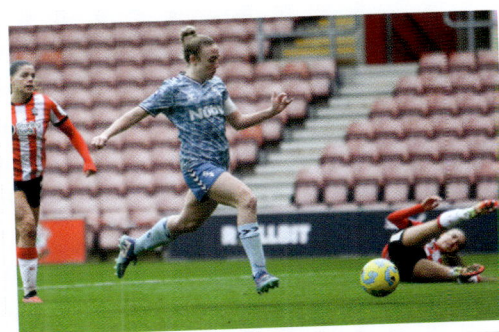

LIBBI MCINNES
VS DURHAM [H]

McInnes volleyed with the outside of her foot into the near corner to cap a slick team move.

The number of nominations for the Men's Goal of the Season award just kept growing as the team kept scoring sensational goals. Wilson Isidor could have had his own Goal of the Season competition as he had three goals shortlisted. However the winner was the goal that was last added to the list after Eliezer Mayenda's April wondergoal at Bristol City.

CHRIS RIGG
VS MIDDLESBROUGH (H)

Sky Bet's Championship Goal of the Month for September. Latching onto a block from a typically mesmerising Patrick Roberts run, Chris combined his quick thinking and quick feet to backheel a derby winner.

DENNIS CIRKIN
VS COVENTRY CITY (H)

Starting the move on the edge of his own box, Cirkin played a one-two with Romaine Mundle inside his own half and motored forward before lashing home a screamer from outside the area.

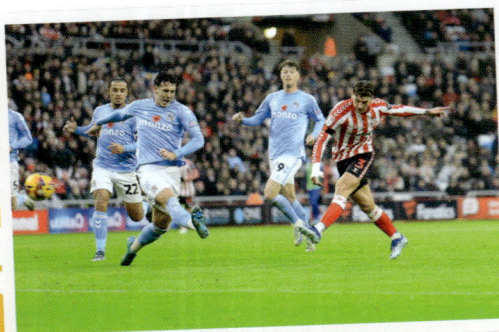

WILSON ISIDOR
VS HULL CITY (A)

Receiving the ball in his own half, Isidor left a vapour trail behind him as he sped almost the length of the pitch before scoring the only goal of the game.

WILSON ISIDOR
VS OXFORD UNITED (H)

An outrageously difficult piece of skill made to look easy, as Wilson volleyed home a ball that dropped over his shoulder from Dan Neil's scooped pass.

JOBE
VS DERBY COUNTY (H)

Jobe collected a loose ball, took a couple of touches, and rocketed home a shot from 25 yards.

WILSON ISIDOR
VS COVENTRY CITY (H)

A spectacular left-footed volley, as Wilson met Romaine Mundle's cross.

TRAI HUME
VS MILLWALL (H)

A cleverly worked corner kick routine. Trading passes with Romaine Mundle, Patrick Roberts floated an inviting ball to the far post from where Trai Hume scored with an expertly controlled volley.

ROMAINE MUNDLE
VS PRESTON NORTH END (H)

Dropped the shoulder to wrong-foot a defender as he cut inside and curled home a spectacular shot from the angle of the penalty area. The goal was the Championship's Goal of the Month for March.

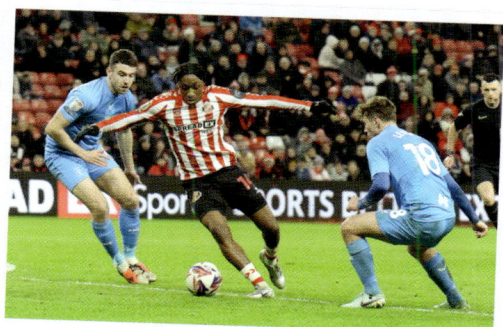

DAN NEIL
VS SWANSEA CITY (A)

Collecting a pass from Jobe, Dan strode forward before arrowing home a beautiful shot from 25 yards.

ENZO LE FÉE
VS LUTON (H)

A magnificent finish from just outside the box after receiving from Trai Hume.

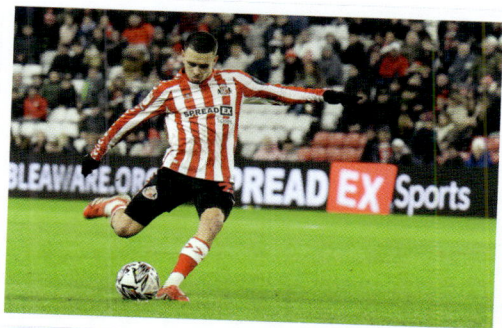

ELIEZER MAYENDA
VS BRISTOL CITY (A)

The Spain Under 21 international collected the ball and ran three-quarters of the length of the pitch with it, single-handedly outmuscling and outpacing the home defence before showing great composure to find the back of the net.

WOMEN'S SUPER LEAGUE 2

Sunderland finished seventh in their league table in 2025. They won eight games, lost eight games and drew three times.

Dale and Jones

This season, Sunderland are aiming to be in the thick of the race for promotion to the Women's Super League with the league Sunderland are in now called Women's Super League 2.

TOP FOUR GAMES

Sunderland 4-3 Bristol City

This was a real thriller. In a dramatic spell of second-half action, the Lasses scored three goals in five minutes to come from 1–2 down to lead 4–2. Although the Robins pulled one back, braces from Eleanor Dale and Katie Kitching secured all three points in front of an excited home crowd.

Bristol City 2-3 Sunderland

These two sides produced another goal fest in the return fixture with Sunderland coming out on top once again. Showing their fighting spirit, the Black Cats clawed their way back into the match after trailing, just as they had done in their home game. This time Ellen Jones and Katy Watson were the goal-scorers. Jones blasted home two volleys before substitute Watson grabbed a dramatic late winner.

Sunderland 2-0 Durham

Sunderland stage most of their games at Eppleton but sometimes play at the Stadium of Light where they pulled in a record crowd of over 15,000 last season. This River Wear derby against Durham was at the main stadium where Libbi McInnes and Amy Goddard got the goals.

Exeter City 1-7 Sunderland

This was a women's Adobe FA Cup game during an excellent cup-run to the quarter-final. After knocking out Huddersfield Town with an emphatic 4-0 score-line Sunderland went even more goal crazy in the west country, smashing Exeter for seven with Ellen Jones getting a hat trick and Eleanor Dale going one better with four goals. The cup run continued with an away win at Portsmouth to take the Lasses into the last eight alongside Women's Super League sides Manchester City, Arsenal, Chelsea, Liverpool, Crystal Palace, Aston Villa and Manchester United with United needing an injury time goal from England star Ella Toone to end Sunderland's determined display as the game finished 3-1.

Celebrating Libbi McInnes' goal vs Durham

GLOBAL GIRL

Sunderland women's Player of the Season Katie Kitching is something of a United Nations midfielder.

Born in Bedale in North Yorkshire, she spent five years at the University of South Florida in the USA, is an international with New Zealand, took part in the 2024 Olympics in Paris and played in Manchester and London before coming to Sunderland in the summer of 2023.

A set-piece specialist, Katie's free kicks – especially from the left flank – are always a major part of Sunderland's attacking threat. Last season KK reached double figures in goal involvements, with her strikes at Charlton and at home to Bristol City being short-listed for the club's Goal of the Season, the latter also being nominated for the league's Goal of the Month. Opponents often felt that sinking feeling having had the Kitching sink thrown at them.

The 27-year-old has been a model of consistency since signing for Sunderland. She has been short-listed for the Player of the Season award in both of her complete campaigns at the club, lifting the award in 2025.

As a girl growing up in North Yorkshire Katie started playing with her dad and brother when she was eight, soon making Ripon City Panthers her first club before spending six years as part of York City's Centre of Excellence. Her talent was spotted by Manchester City who signed Kitching after she had helped York knock Manchester United out of the FA Youth Cup. She represented City in the FA Women's Super League reserve league before going to study in the USA.

During her time in America, Kitching played for the South Florida Bulls where she developed as a player. In 2017 she started nine games and came off the bench in a further four, scoring her first goal with a winner at ECU in September. Starting to make a name for herself, shortly after that goal Katie was named the American Athletic Conference Rookie of the Week and was also selected for the Conference All-Rookie team. Progress continued the following year when Katie played 19 times, all but three of them as starts, and contributed three assists. The upward trajectory carried on in 2019 when she was chosen for an UTSA All-Tournament team. This was in a season where only one of her 21 appearances was as a sub and she got on the scoresheet against Wake Forest. In her final two seasons at South Florida she made the AAC Honour Roll on both occasions, eventually totalling 85 games for the university. This was the third highest in the university's history. Over the course of Katie's time there she helped her team to six Conference titles while studying Health Sciences.

After completing her studies Katie returned to England in January 2022, becoming a professional footballer with London City Lionesses for whom she played 17 times before coming to Sunderland. After hitting the ground running with Sunderland Katie found herself called up by New Zealand who she qualifies for because her mam is from that country. Debuting in 2023, she played at the 2024 Olympics, scoring in France against Zambia in a warm-up game for the tournament. During the same year she also netted against the Solomon Islands in an Olympic Qualifying match and also scored against Thailand in New Zealand as family and friends watched what the global girl could do.

Katie Kitching

CENTRE CIRCLE

In each section of this ball there is the name of a Sunderland player but every player has a letter missing. Each player has the same letter missing. Can you work out the players and the missing letter?

1 A A E I L J S

2 D N I Z R E A Y

3 E L N U K O I N

4 A L A M I N C S K

5 H R A U T I M

6 O J L E D E H L

FIND THE ANSWERS ON PAGE 61.

SPOT THE DIFFERENCE

Can you spot eight differences from when Sunderland took on Real Betis?

FIND THE ANSWERS ON PAGE 61

SAMSON SHOWS YOU HOW TO MAKE

THE PURRFECT BIRTHDAY CARD

It's always extra special if you take the trouble to make someone a birthday card. Samson shows you how easy it is.

YOU WILL NEED

- 1 sheet white card 30cm x 21cm
- White paper
- Coloured pencils or felt tips
- Glue stick
- Scissors (be careful – get an adult to help you)
- Sellotape
- Pencil

STEP 2

Draw a picture of Samson on a sheet of paper – he's here for you to copy! Make this about ¾ of the size of your card. Colour this in and carefully cut it out.

STEP 3

Stick your picture onto the front of the card. Leave a space at the top to write Samson Says in large letters.

STEP 1

Turn your card so that the long sides are at the top and the bottom then fold in half sideways.

STEP 4

Inside the card will be a surprise – a pop-up back cat!

Draw the shape on a piece of paper. You can draw your own or copy our black cat here. Colour it in and carefully cut it out.

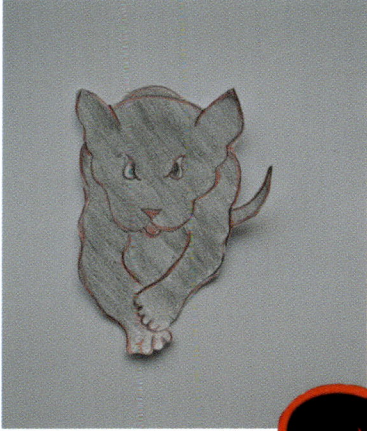

STEP 5

Cut a narrow strip of paper approximately 10cm long and make it into a ring and stick the ends together. Stick this ring onto the back of the black cat.

STEP 6

Stick a piece of Sellotape through the back of the ring to fasten it to the inside of the card. You should now see the black cat leap out! Write Happy Birthday in large letters along the top.

SAMSON, born 1994

SAMSON AND DELILAH

DELILAH, born 1998

Samson and Delilah are black cats who are Sunderland's mascots. Sunderland have had black cats as mascots for well over a hundred years, for example when Sunderland played in the FA Cup final in 1913 many supporters had black cat decorations.

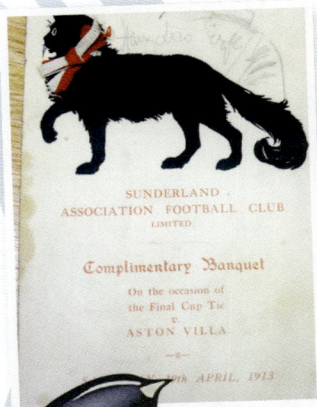

SUNDERLAND
ASSOCIATION FOOTBALL CLUB
LIMITED

Complimentary Banquet

On the occasion of
the Final Cup Tie
v.
ASTON VILLA

19th APRIL, 1913

Sunderland first got the nickname of the Black Cats when they moved to an area of Sunderland called Roker where a local look-out post on the sea front had become known as the Black Cat Battery.

But when did Samson and Delilah come along at the football club? The Black Cats officially became the club's nickname in the late 1990s after the club moved to the Stadium of Light. At their previous ground, Roker Park, they had been known as the Rokerites. A vote was held amongst supporters for a new nickname and the Black Cats won.

During the 1980s sometimes cartoon versions of black cats appeared on some pieces of club merchandise but these black cats did not have a name. In 1984 there were drawings of a black cat on Roker Bingo tickets but this just a simple black cat and definitely not Samson or Delilah who were not yet born! in 1989 the club even produced and sold inflatable black cats such as the ones pictured in 1989 here with Sunderland's centre-forward of the time, Thomas Hauser.

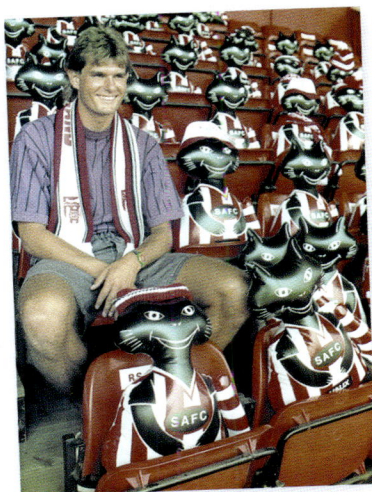

Samson is older than Delilah. It was in 1994 season that the team's strip started to have the name Samson on the front. This was because at the time the club's sponsors were the famous Sunderland brewers Vaux. One of their beers was called Samson because in the bible the character Samson has tremendous strength. Soon after Samson started to appear on the team's shirts the match programme started to show cartoon images of a black cat wearing a strip with the name Samson on, although up to this point the cat was not known as Samson, he simply had on a strip with the Samson sponsor name on.

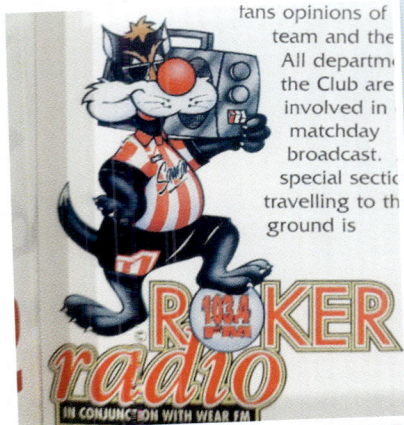

One of the cartoon images of the cat had him holding a radio because he was supposed to be listening to Roker Radio. This was the club's own programmes at Roker Park.

During the summer of 1994 SAFC's sponsorship with Vaux was extended and was announced that this would involve advertising, promotion and community projects. It was as part of this that Samson started to become more noticeable. On 22 October 1994 the Sunderland Echo first gave a mention of "Sunderland's new mascot" actually being called Samson.

The following month the first photograph of the

Samson mascot – as opposed to a cartoon – appeared in the match programme.

From then on photos of Samson at the match or community events became common and he started to be regularly referred to as Samson the cat as the name caught on.

Samson never had a partner when Sunderland still played at Roker Park. He was nearly four when Delilah came along in 1998, the year after the Stadium of Light opened. The Sunderland Echo revealed Samson's new female partner in April 1998 a few days after her first appearance at the Stadium of Light which was for a 2-1 win against Bury.

The Echo asked Samson what he thought of having his new partner. He purred, "Being in the tunnel with Delilah is scarier than being in the tunnel with Vinnie Jones". Vinnie Jones was then the game's toughest hard man. Delilah also features in the bible but to put it mildly she isn't always nice to Samson! They seem to have become a bit friendlier now.

Mine, mine, mine Delilah! Mascot Samson finds his stadium soulmate

Echo, Thursday April 2 1998

Picture by Malcolm Murray No. 45785

THAT'S MY GIRL: Dance City artistic director Janet Archer puts Samson and Delilah through their paces.

THE Echo today unmasks Sunderland AFC's new mascot Delilah, and reveals why, why, way she wanted the job so much.
The feline friend for long-standing mascot Samson is trainee teacher Fiona Williamson, 25, from Gordon Drive, East Boldon.
And thanks to lessons at professional dance studio, Dance City, in Newcastle, she and Samson will be ...

letter complimenting the club on the excellent facilities for women at the new stadium, but saying that in this age of equality they should have a female cat, but I lost my bottle.
"Then Eric Gates said the very same thing on the radio and the club advertised for the job. I was terrified in case someone else got it.
"I pestered and pestered the club until they gave me the job and here ...

a wiggle if you make yourself known."
Fiona plans to continue her catty career once she secures a permanent teaching post, but said she'll be keeping it quiet from her pupils.
Purring with delight about his new feline friend, Samson, alias Tony Dawson, said: "I feel like the cat that got the cream, it's purrrfect.

STADIUM STATUES

There are two statues at the Stadium of Light...

THE STOKOE STATUE

- Bob Stokoe was Sunderland's manager when they won the FA Cup in 1973.

- He had taken over mid-way through the season with the team struggling in what is now the Championship.

- Stokoe transformed the team who went on to win the cup in sensational style.

- Amongst others, cup favourites Manchester City and Arsenal were knocked out by Sunderland.

- Leeds were one of the top teams of the time and were the cup holders but were beaten by Sunderland in the final.

- Three years later Sunderland won what is now the Championship under Stokoe.

- After winning the FA Cup he was nicknamed 'The Messiah' by supporters.

- One of Stokoe's famous sayings was, "Until you've seen football on the north-east coast, you've never seen it."

Bob Stokoe's daughter made a speech on the day her dad's statue was unveiled.

THE FANS' STATUE

- Supporters are so important at Sunderland that a statue of fans has pride of place near the main entrance of the Stadium of Light.

- The Fans' Statue shows a family of supporters with a man, a woman and two children.

- The noise from Sunderland's old stadium Roker Park was known worldwide as "The Roker Roar."

- Next to the Fans' Statue are plaques in honour of supporters who have tragically died in road accidents travelling to matches and also a plaque dedicated to the players who lost their lives in the World Wars.

- The Fans' Statue is the centre-piece of a memorial garden being created there to honour Sunderland supporters who have passed away.

YOU'RE BOOKED

Hopefully you are enjoying reading the Sunderland annual. Have you read any other books on Sunderland? There are lots of them. Many of these books are the life stories of players or managers. Life stories are called biographies. If the book has been written by the person themself (or by a writer who has spoken at length to the player or manager) they are called autobiographies.

NIALL QUINN & SUPERKEV

In the early years of the Stadium of Light Sunderland had the best strikers in the country. In 1999-2000 Kevin Phillips won the Premier League Golden Boot and the European Golden Shoe as Europe's top scorer. Superkev scored 30 Premier League goals with his centre-forward partner Niall Quinn setting up many of them and scoring 14 of his own in the same season. Kevin Phillips brought out a book called, '**Second Time Around**'. This hardback book was soon reprinted as a paperback with a couple of extra chapters and a new title, '**Strikingly Different**'. Quinn's book is simply called, '**Niall Quinn. The Autobiography**'.

DICKIE ORD

Richard Ord was a very popular player who operated as a defender or midfielder and made almost 300 appearances for Sunderland, finishing in 1998. Manchester United's Eric Cantona was a superstar at the time so whenever fans chanted about Ord they chanted, '**Who needs Cantona when we've got Dickie Ord**' and that chant became the title of a highly entertaining biography.

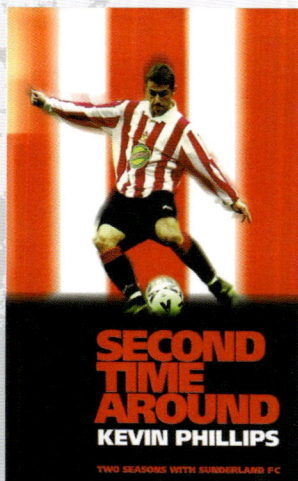

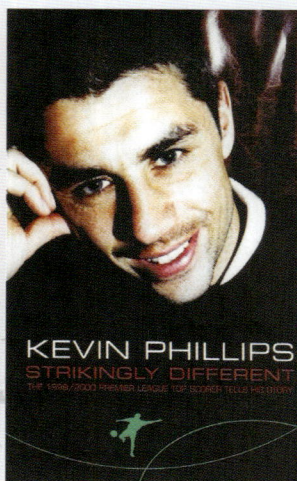

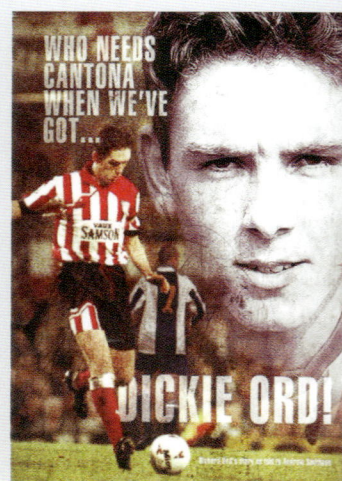

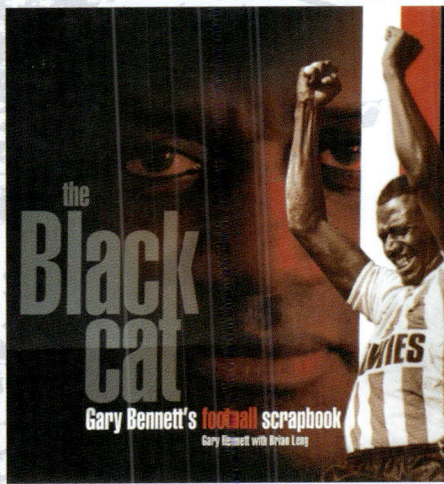

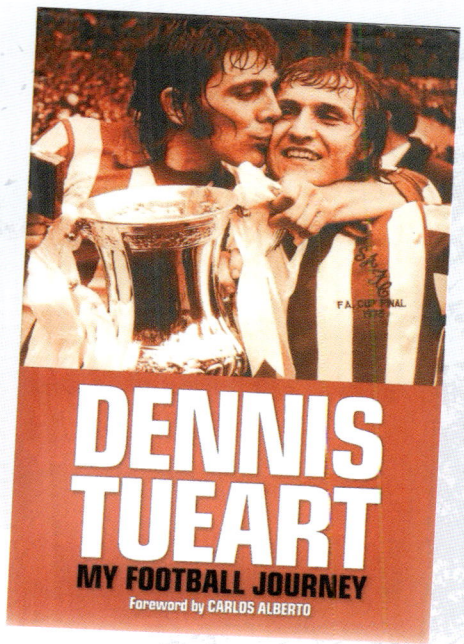

GARY BENNETT

These days Gary Bennett is known to younger supporters as the radio summariser of Sunderland's games on local radio. As a player in the 1980s and 1990s "Benno" captained the team and was twice Player of the Season. His book is called 'The Black Cat – Gary Bennett's Football Scrapbook'.

LEN SHACKLETON

In his day Len Shackleton was even more of a superstar than Eric Cantona became. "Shack", as everyone called him, played so long ago it might have been before your grandparents were born. "Shack" stopped playing in 1957. As well as being an incredible footballer he was a person who let everyone know his opinions. Famously he had a chapter in his autobiography. 'The Clown Prince of Soccer' which he called 'The average director's knowledge of football' – in which he deliberately left a blank page.

DENNIS TUEART

Dennis Tueart played in the 1973 FA Cup final for Sunderland. He had a brilliant career, starring for Manchester City and England. At one point he was signed by New York Cosmos to replace the Brazil megastar Pele! Dennis donated all the profits from his autobiography, 'My Football Journey' to charity.

BOB STOKOE

As well as players, sometimes managers produce biographies. Dennis Tueart's manager when Sunderland won the cup in 1973 was Bob Stokoe. Stokoe's biography is called, 'Northern and Proud' and like the many books of former Sunderland players and managers it is well worth reading if you want to learn more about the history of SAFC.

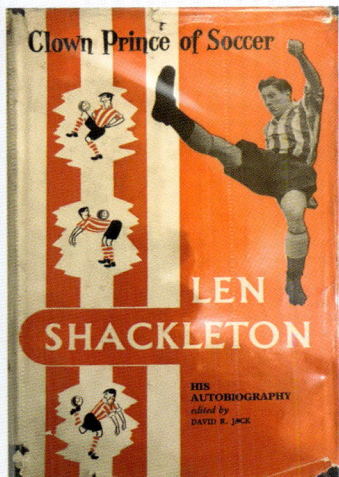

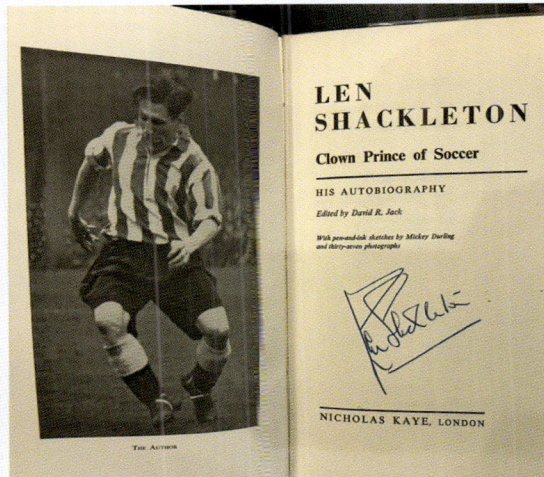

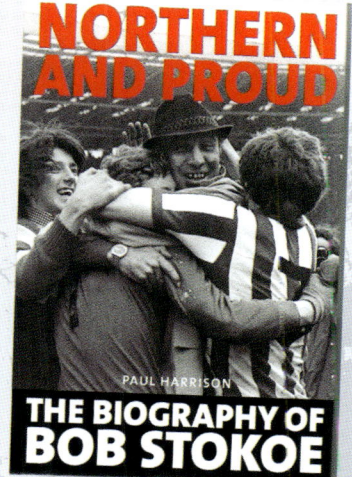

TEST YOURSELF ON 2025

How much attention have you been paying to SAFC in 2025? See how many of these questions on Sunderland in 2025 you can get right.

1. Who scored Sunderland's first goal of 2025?

2. Who are Sunderland scheduled to face in the final game of 2025?

3. Who did Sunderland play in the Play-off semi-finals?

4. Who did Sunderland sign in January after having him on loan earlier in the season?

5. Who was the midfielder brought in on loan from AS Roma?

6. Who did Brighton sign from Sunderland in the summer?

7. Which Australian player was named Hibernian's Young Player of the Year during his loan with the Edinburgh club?

8. Eliezer Mayenda won the award for Men's Goal of the Season. Who did he score it against?

9. Who was named Men's Player and Players' Player of the Season?

10. Who was named Women's Player of the Season?

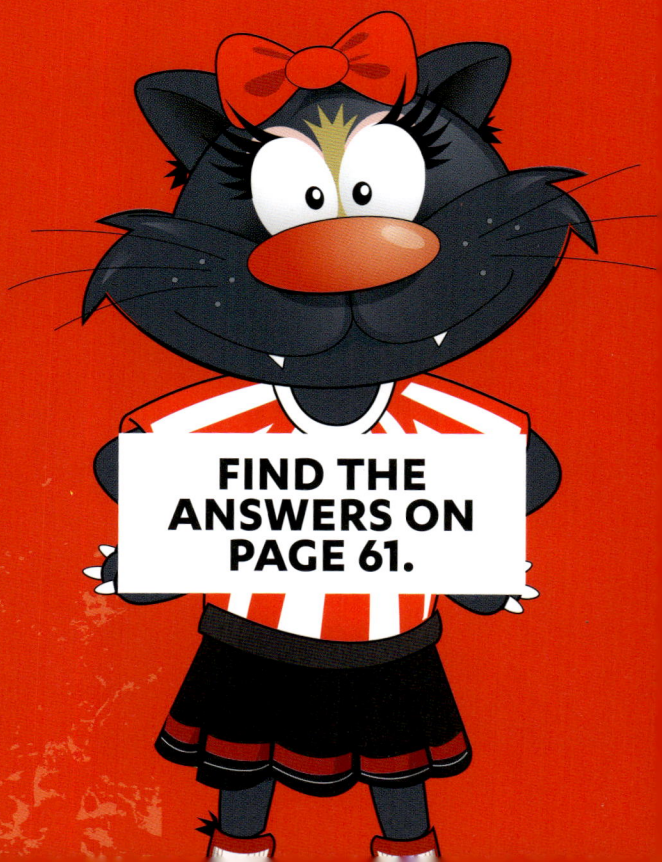

FIND THE ANSWERS ON PAGE 61.

TEST YOURSELF ON SUNDERLAND'S HISTORY

1. Who is Sunderland's record appearance maker?
   A. Luke O'Nien
   B. Jimmy Montgomery
   C. Raich Carter

2. How many games did Sunderland's record appearance maker play?
   A. 1,000
   B. 527
   C. 627

3. How many times have Sunderland been champions of England?
   A. 0
   B. 3
   C. 6

4. Which of these teams have Sunderland never played at Wembley?
   A. Leeds United
   B. Aston Villa
   C. Liverpool

5. Which of these players has scored for Sunderland at Wembley?
   A. Ian Porterfield
   B. Charlie Wyke
   C. Darren Bent

6. Before they ever played in red and white, what was the original colour of Sunderland's shirts?
   A. Blue
   B. White
   C. All red

7. Which player has won most international caps while with Sunderland?
   A. John O'Shea
   B. Charlie Hurley
   C. Seb Larsson

8. Which of these former Sunderland managers have never managed an international team?
   A. Sam Allardyce
   B. Dick Advocaat
   C. Jack Ross

9. Who has scored most goals for Sunderland since the end of World War Two in 1945?
   A. Kevin Phillips
   B. Gary Rowell
   C. Len Shackleton

10. How many times did the player with the most goals for Sunderland since the end of World War Two score for the club?
    A. 110
    B. 120
    C. 130

FIND THE ANSWERS ON PAGE 61

SIMON
ADINGRA

ANSWERS

PAGES 12

ON THE BALL
1) Luke O'Nien
2) Wilson Isidor
3) Milan Aleksic

CORNERED
Granit Xhaka
Enzo Le Fée
Eliezer Mayenda
Omar Alderete

FACT OR FIB
1) Fact: Ballard was born in Stevenage, near London.
2) Fact: Hjelde was born in Nottingham.
3) Fib: Cirkin was born in Dublin, in Ireland.

SPOT THE SCORE-LINE
1) Sunderland 4 -0 Sheffield Wednesday
2) Middlesbrough 2 –3 Sunderland
3) Portsmouth 1 – 3 Sunderland
4) Sunderland 2 – 0 Luton Town

PAGES 32 & 33

SPOT THE STADIUM
1. Anfielc
2. Craven Cottage
3. Emirates
4. Molineux Stadium
5. Stadium of Light
6. The Etihad

WHO IS IT?
1) Aji Alese
2) Dan Ballard
3) Eliezer Mayenda
4) Wilson Isidor

PAGE 48

CENTRE CIRCLE
The missing letter is E.
1) Aji Alese
2) Eliezer Mayenda
3) Luke O'Nien
4) Milan Aleksić
5) Trai Hume
6) Leo Hjelde

PAGES 58 & 59

TEST YOURSELF ON 2025
1 Eliezer Mayenda
2 Manchester City
3 Coventry City
4 Wilson Isidor
5 Enzo Le Fée
6 Tommy Watson
7 Nectar Triantis
8 Bristol City
9 Trai Hume
10 Katie Kitching

SAFC HISTORY
1) B Jimmy Montgomery
2) C 627
3) C 6
4) B Aston Villa
5) A Ian Porterfield
6) A Blue
7) C Seb Larsson
8) C Jack Ross
9) A Kevin Phillips
10) 130

PAGE 49
SPOT THE DIFFERENCE